RORY McILROY

BY PAUL LOGOTHETIS

SportsZone

An Imprint of Abdo Publishing
abdopublishing.com

THIS BOOK CONTAINS
RECYCLED MATERIALS

Cover Photo: Fred Kfoury III/Icon Sportswire/AP Images, cover
Interior Images: Fred Kfoury III/Icon Sportswire/AP Images, 1; Stephen Hindley/ AP Images, 4; John Locher/AP Images, 7; Charles Rex Arbogast/AP Images, 9; Peter Morrison/AP Images, 11, 15, 27; Kin Cheung/AP Images, 12; Gerry Broome/AP Images, 16; Matt Slocum/AP Images, 19; Evan Vucci/AP Images, 21; Mike Frey/Rex Features/ AP Images, 22; Brian Lawless/Press Association/AP Images, 25; Jeff Moreland/Icon Sportswire/AP Images, 29

Editor: Nick Rebman
Series Designer: Craig Hinton

Library of Congress Control Number: 2015931754

Cataloging-in-Publication Data

Logothetis, Paul.
 Rory McIlroy: Golf champion / Paul Logothetis.
   p. cm. -- (Playmakers)
Includes bibliographical references and index.
ISBN 978-1-62403-838-9
1. McIlroy, Rory, 1989- --Juvenile literature. 2. Golfers--Northern Ireland--Biography--Juvenile literature.   I. Title.
796.352092--dc23
[B]   2015931754

TABLE OF CONTENTS

Rory McIlroy

CHAPTER 1

BOY WONDER

Rory McIlroy stared down the 10th fairway. The sun was setting. He was playing in the 2014 Professional Golfers' Association (PGA) Championship. He was three shots behind the leader. It was the final round. His chance of winning the tournament seemed to be slipping away.

McIlroy lined up his 3-wood. He hit a near perfect shot. Then he made his eagle putt. That put him within one shot of the lead. After that he made

McIlroy takes a shot on the final hole of the DP World Tour Championship in Dubai.

two more birdies. His opponents could not keep up. McIlroy was now leading by one shot. He just had to make par on the final hole.

It was nearly dark. McIlroy sank his putt for par. He had won his fourth major title. And he was only 25 years old. Only three players had been younger than him when they won their fourth major.

McIlroy competed against a robot in 2013. It was for a funny TV commercial. McIlroy and the robot took turns trying to hit targets. The targets were washing machines. The robot teased McIlroy. It moved the machines. The two were tied before the last target. But McIlroy hit his shot perfectly and won the contest.

Rory's father Gerry introduced him to golf at a young age. Gerry was already a very good player. And he saw that Rory had a lot of talent. By the age of two, Rory could hit the ball 40 yards. He was already showing his potential.

Rory's parents did all they could to encourage his love of golf. Their sacrifice gave Rory the chance to develop his skills.

McIlroy poses with his trophy after winning the 2014 PGA Championship in the dark.

Gerry worked three jobs. He worked 100-hour weeks. One of his jobs was at a golf course. He even scrubbed toilets and showers. It was all to save up money for Rory. Gerry wanted his son to be able to fly to the United States and play in tournaments. The McIlroys knew the sacrifice would be worth it.

Rory was born in Holywood, Northern Ireland. That is in the United Kingdom. Rory's family members played at Holywood Golf Club. His father and uncle had both won the Holywood club championship. Rory wanted to join the club, too. But he was only seven years old. The club rules said players had to be 12 to join. Rory's golf game was so good that the club changed its rules. Now Rory could be a member.

When Rory was 15, he agreed to play golf for East Tennessee State University. But after winning more tournaments the next year, Rory changed his mind. He decided to keep playing in Europe.

Rory was passionate about getting better at golf. He even practiced his chipping inside the house. Rory lined up balls in the kitchen. He aimed for the washing machine. He chipped one ball after another down the hallway.

McIlroy, *left*, speaks to Tiger Woods during a 2012 tournament in Indiana.

Soon people started to hear about Rory's skill. His name became famous in Northern Ireland. He was invited onto a TV show to perform his chip trick. Rory was eight years old. He lined up in front of the washing machine. His first chip missed to the left. His second shot went too high. Chipping was the best part of Rory's game. So he kept trying. His third shot hit the rim and bounced out.

When McIlroy was growing up, Tiger Woods was one of his heroes. McIlroy always dreamed of getting the chance to meet Woods and play with him. They are both sponsored by Nike. So they were able to meet and become friends. Woods was impressed by McIlroy's athleticism, confidence, and consistency.

Rory finally made the chip on his fourth try. He had a big smile on his face. He told the audience he wanted to become a professional golfer. Rory's parents showed their early sacrifice here, too. Gerry missed an important golf event so Rory could be on TV. Rory was learning about the value of sacrifice early on.

Rory shoots for the green at a 2007 tournament in Northern Ireland.

Rory's practice was paying off. He scored a hole in one at the age of nine. At the age of 10, he won a world championship for junior players.

CHAPTER 2

GOING PRO

ory McIlroy knew the kind of shot every golf club could produce. He could hit shots that many experienced golfers struggled to hit. His swing was very fast for a teenager. This allowed him to hit the ball farther.

In 2005, Rory became the youngest winner of the Irish Amateur Championship. He was only 16 years old. He was already playing in professional tournaments, too.

Rory McIlroy walks down the fairway at the Omega Mission Hills World Cup in China in 2009.

Rory was on an incredible run. But he had doubts sometimes. One day after winning a tournament, Rory was not sure he wanted to keep golfing. It took up all of his time and energy. He felt like he was missing out on the life of a regular kid. He told his father that he wanted to quit the game. They talked about it for hours. Rory decided to take a break from golf. But after three days without playing, he missed the game too much. Rory quickly picked up his clubs again.

McIlroy grew up without much money. But his success has made him richer than he ever imagined. In his first six years on the PGA Tour, he earned more than $23 million.

Rory became the world's top amateur player when he was 17. It was the same year that he won the Silver Medal at the British Open. This award is given to the best player who is not a professional. He was 18 when he decided to stop being an amateur. Some golfers play for a whole year before they qualify as a professional. Others never make it. But Rory qualified

A seventeen-year-old Rory McIlroy tees off at Royal County Down golf club in 2007.

after only two tournaments. Before Rory, no one in Europe had earned that chance at such a young age. Now he was ready to take on the world's best players.

Rory McIlroy

WHAT A START

Rory McIlroy did not waste any time in making an impact on the golf world. He won his first international title only a few months into his career.

McIlroy had already received a lot of attention. He was a golf prodigy, which means he was great from a young age. People said he could rival Tiger Woods to be the world's best golfer. Expectations were very high.

McIlroy celebrates after sinking his last putt at the Quail Hollow Championship in 2010.

At first, McIlroy played better in Europe than in North America. He was more comfortable playing closer to home. He knew many of the golfers. He also knew the courses. This meant he was more relaxed when playing in Europe. He was still new to playing in the United States. So it took him longer to create the same feeling he had in Europe.

McIlroy is not a large man. But he is one of the most powerful hitters in the game. He was the third-longest driver in 2014. His average score of 68.8 per round was the best in the PGA Tour. He finished in the top 25 in all 17 tour events he entered in 2014.

McIlroy played poorly at the 2010 Masters. He did not make the cut. That meant he did not score well enough to play in the later rounds of the tournament. But in the next tournament, he made history. At the Quail Hollow Championship, it looked like he would miss the cut. Then he shot a 62 in the final round. That was 10-under par. McIlroy was not even 21 yet. Even so, he was becoming a household name. And he was playing like a champion.

McIlroy shows his disappointment after missing a putt at the 2011 Masters.

For McIlroy, 2011 was an important year. He was playing well. And now it was time for the Masters. This tournament lasts four days. McIlroy was great during the first three days. He led by four shots. At age 21, he had a chance to become the second-youngest Masters champion after Woods.

It was time for the final day of the tournament. McIlroy still led with only nine holes to go. But then everything changed. McIlroy tried to play differently than he normally did.

He took risks. He played shots he normally would not try. He was too aggressive and lost his focus. He made mistakes. He went from first to fifteenth.

McIlroy was very disappointed. The pressure had gotten to him. And he lost the Masters because of it. But he decided to use that experience to become a better golfer. He never again wanted to play how others expected him to play. He wanted to do things his own way.

The Ryder Cup is played every two years. The 12 best US players compete against the 12 best European players. In 2012 McIlroy almost missed his tee off after mixing up his start time. He needed a police escort to arrive just before the match started. He still won.

Two months later at the US Open, McIlroy won his first major. Majors are the four most important tournaments in golf. McIlroy won by eight shots. He beat Woods's record for lowest score at the US Open. And he became the youngest US Open champion since Bobby Jones in 1923.

McIlroy smiles as he holds up his trophy at the 2011 US Open.

McIlroy's confidence returned. One year later, he won his second major championship. McIlroy looked unstoppable. He won the 2012 PGA Championship by a record eight shots. He even wore a red shirt for the last round. That was Woods's trademark move. It signaled that McIlroy was up to the challenge of beating the best. He was 23 years and three months old when he won his second major. Even Woods had not won two majors at such a young age.

Rory McIlroy

CHAPTER 4

DISTRACTIONS AND TRIUMPHS

Rory McIlroy's success meant many changes in his life. He signed a contract with Nike. That meant Nike would use McIlroy to sell and promote its products. This made McIlroy very rich. He was the top-ranked player in the world. There was more attention on him wherever he played. McIlroy's move to Nike meant he had to change clubs. He also had to do more publicity work. These distractions took a toll on his game.

McIlroy shoots out of a sand trap at a 2014 tournament in Australia.

McIlroy struggled to stay consistent. Things got very bad at the Honda Classic in 2013. McIlroy walked off the course without finishing. He had won that tournament the year before.

McIlroy said he could not concentrate anymore. He made excuses. It almost seemed like McIlroy was a teenager again. He was unsure if golf was his passion.

After winning the PGA Championship, McIlroy donated more than $1 million to open a cancer center. It allows children and their families to get a break from their suffering. McIlroy hoped the project would be the first of many around the world.

Going into 2014, McIlroy had fallen to number six in the world rankings. He'd had a year to forget. Many people thought he would not be able to bounce back. But they were very wrong.

McIlroy attends the opening of Daisy Lodge, a cancer center for children.

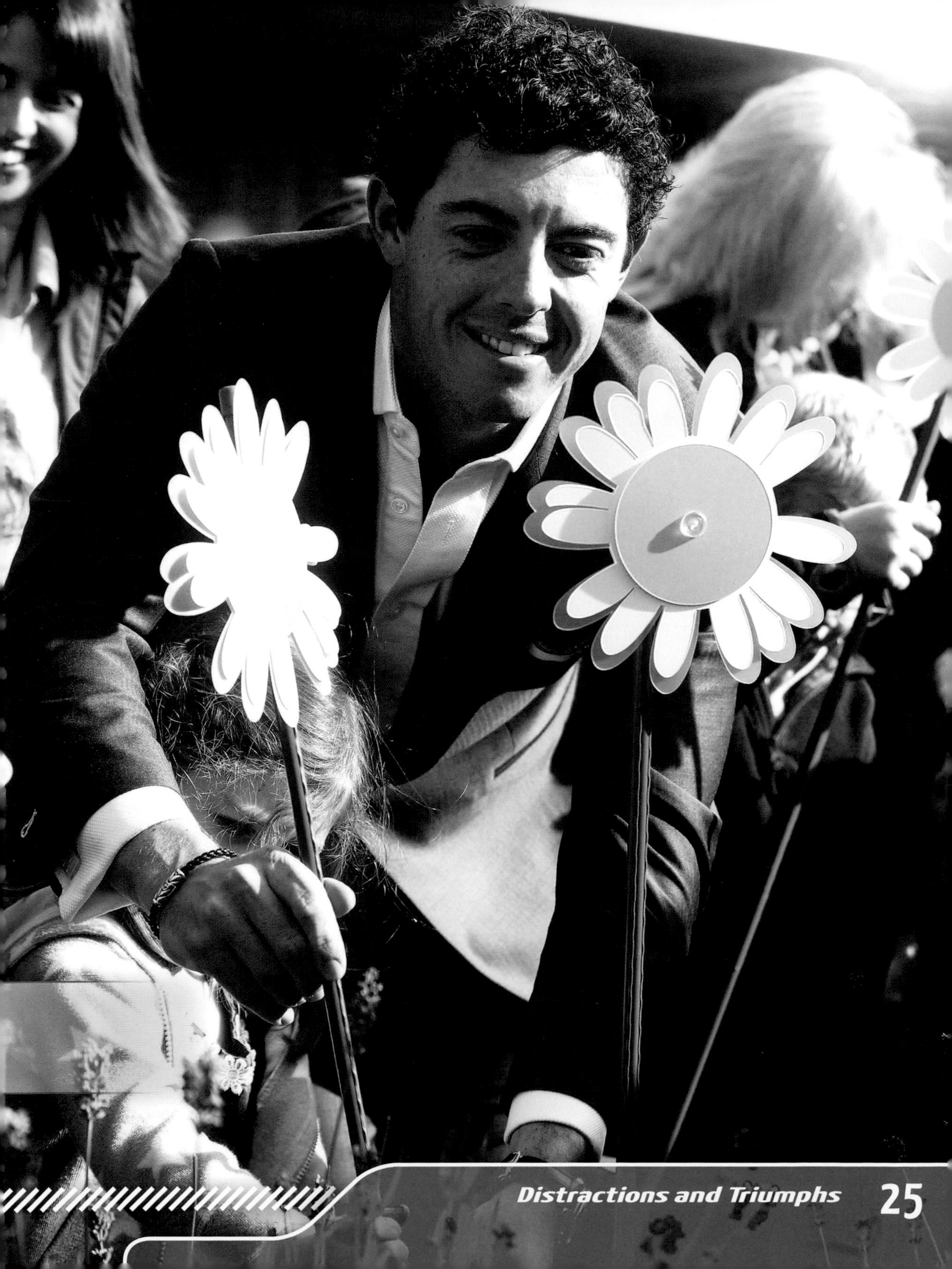

McIlroy was the best golfer in the world in 2014. He had made major changes in his life. He put more focus on golf. He spent more time training. McIlroy became one of the strongest players on the PGA Tour. He cut his curly hair short. He looked more serious. But his smile and freckles always remained.

His turnaround started at the Honda Classic. One year earlier he had walked off the course. This time he made a birdie putt on the 18th hole. This shot forced a playoff. He lost the tournament, but his confidence was high.

McIlroy nearly married tennis star Caroline Wozniacki. They were together for two years. McIlroy proposed on New Year's Eve. Later, he realized he was not ready for marriage and canceled the wedding.

McIlroy called golf legend Jack Nicklaus later that summer. He asked for advice. Many consider Nicklaus the best golfer of all time. He won a record 18 majors. Nicklaus's advice did not help McIlroy win the US Open. But it did help him win the next three tournaments. That included his first British Open trophy.

McIlroy hugs his mother, Rosie, after winning the 2014 British Open.

McIlroy led from start to finish. His mother celebrated with him on the 18th hole. They both cried tears of joy.

McIlroy won his next tournament, too. After that he played in the PGA Championship. That is another major. And he won it in near darkness.

McIlroy had made history. He was number one in the world. He was also the first European to win three different majors. He was the fourth golfer in the last 100 years to win four majors by the age of 25. But most of all, McIlroy had found the joy of golf again. His smile beamed across his face. It reminded everyone of when he was a kid chipping balls into the washing machine.

McIlroy got his name in the *Guinness Book of World Records* in 2014. His total score at the US Open for 72 holes was 268. That was the lowest in tournament history. So was his 16-under par total.

McIlroy played very well in the summer of 2014. People even called it the "Summer of Rory." But he wanted more. He knew that only five players had won all four majors. He wanted to be the sixth.

McIlroy lines up a putt during a practice round at the 2014 Masters.

FUN FACTS AND QUOTES

- McIlroy spends a lot of time in his pool, hot tub, and personal gym. His trophy room holds all of his prizes. But he also left some empty spaces for the trophies he still wants to win.

- McIlroy lists soccer as one of his favorite sports besides golf. His favorite team is Manchester United in England. After McIlroy won the 2014 British Open, Manchester United honored him at its Old Trafford stadium.

- *"Rory is going to have a great career, there is no question about that. He has got all the components. He is a great kid. He is humble when he needs to be and confident when he needs to be confident. He's got a great swing. He looks a little cocksure when he walks, which you need to have. I like it."* —Jack Nicklaus commenting on McIlroy after the 2011 US Open

- McIlroy has some talent for tennis, too. He once played a point against tennis champion Maria Sharapova. It was just for fun. And McIlroy won the point. He sent Sharapova a lob that she hit wide.

- McIlroy is well known for hitting big drives. At the Scottish Open in 2014, he hit his drive so perfectly that it rolled onto the green of the 436-yard hole. McIlroy set a course record with that round.

WEBSITES

To learn more about Playmakers, visit **booklinks.abdopublishing.com**. These links are routinely monitored and updated to provide the most current information available.

GLOSSARY

birdie
When you score 1-under par on a hole.

British Open
The third major of the season. It is always played in the United Kingdom.

eagle
When you score 2-under par on a hole.

majors
The four most important tournaments in golf.

make the cut
Get a score that is good enough to take part in the final rounds of a tournament.

Masters
The first major of the season. It is played at Augusta National golf course in Georgia.

par
The score a good golfer should shoot on a hole.

PGA Championship
The fourth and last major of the season. It is always played in the United States.

PGA Tour
The organization that gives professionals the chance to play on a North American golf tour.

round
Eighteen holes of golf.

US Open
The second major of the season. It is always played in the United States.

FURTHER RESOURCES

Carr, Aaron. *Golf*. New York: AV2 by Weigl, 2013.

Gifford, Clive. *Golf*. Mankato, MN: Sea-to-Sea, 2010.

McClellan, Ray. *Golf*. Minneapolis: Bellwether Media, 2011.